# AN HISTORICAL GLANCE AT THE BROTHERHOOD OF THE HOLY SEPULCHER

By

RAPHAEL HAWAWEENY
LATE BISHOP OF BROOKLYN
Originally Written & Published in 1893

Translated

By

Archpriest Michel Najim, Ph.D.

ΩAKWOOD ΠUBLICATIONS

# AN HISTORICAL GLANCE AT THE BROTHERHOOD OF THE HOLY SEPULCHER

By
RAPHAEL HAWAWEENY
LATE BISHOP OF BROOKLYN
Translated
By
Archpriest Michel Najim, Ph.D.

ALL RIGHTS RESERVED
© 1996 by
The Task Force to support the Orthodox Christians in the Patriarchate of Jerusalem

Oakwood Publications
3827 Bluff St.
Torrance, California 90505-6359
Telephone & Fax (310) 378-9245
ISBN No. 1-879038-31-5

Written under the Pseudonym: Sheikh 'Abd El Ahad Eshshafi. Beirut, 1893, Derek Hopwood,
COVER LAYOUT: Victoria Graphics, Orange, CA
GRAPHICS: IconoGraphics Electronic Byzantine Clip Art Collection by TheoLogic Systems.
EDITORIAL SUPPORT: Oakwood Publications, Torrance, CA
PRINTER: KNI, Inc., Anaheim, CA

Bishop Raphael Hawaweeny
1860 - 1915

# CONTENTS

Prologue, by Father Michel Najim ...... VII

Introduction ........................ 1

The Establishment of the Brotherhood of the Holy Sepulcher ..................... 7

The Brotherhood of the Holy Sepulcher and the Holy Land .................... 27

The Brotherhood of the Holy Sepulcher and the Income of the Patriarchate of Jerusalem  39

The Brotherhood of the Holy Sepulcher and the Indigenous Children of the Church of Jerusalem ........................ 47

The Brotherhood of the Holy Sepulcher and its Religious and Moral Condition ........ 57

Conclusion ....................... 67

## PROLOGUE

The Task Force to support the Orthodox Christians in the Patriarchate of Jerusalem was born on Thursday, September 22, 1994, at the home of Doctor and Mrs. George Madanat in the state of California, U.S.A.

All the attendees expressed their concern about the situation of the Orthodox Patriarchate of Jerusalem, Palestine, which includes all of Palestine (Jerusalem, the West Bank, etc. . .) and Jordan, and described the suffering of the indigenous Orthodox people in their own Church under the domination of a few non-indigenous monks. They stated that this kind of foreign domination contradicts faith and Canon Law. They described the deteriorating situation caused by the misconduct of the Patriarch and the bishops, and expressed their alarm for the suffering of the indigenous Christians in the Holy Land.

Following this historic meeting, the First International Conference of the Task Force was held May 12-14, 1995 at the Antiochian Village in Ligonier, Pennsylvania.

The following were the resolutions of that conference:

A - Actions which would make overall changes in the Patriarchate of Jerusalem so as to bring it back to uniformity with the administrative practices of the Holy Orthodox Church.

B - Actions which would reverse the ever declining witness of Orthodoxy under the past and continuing corrupt practices of the Patriarch and the Hierarchy.

The delegates unanimously and strongly condemn the following:

1 - The total abdication of spiritual, educational and material responsibilities toward the flock by the Hierarchy.

2 - The exploitation of church resources and the mismanagement of Church affairs without accountability.

3 - The unjustified sale and long term lease of the Holy Places and other priceless Church properties.

4 - The discrimination against indigenous clergy by preventing their elevation to the level of hierarchs, their harassment and the ignoring of their needs.

5 - The ordination of non-qualified priests.

6 - The abandonment of Orthodox parochial schools which has forced thousands of Orthodox students to transfer to Catholic and Protestant schools, leading directly to the proselytization of their families.

The delegates unanimously and strongly demand the following:

1 - That Patriarchs and primates of all autocephalous churches, and in particular his Holiness the Ecumenical Patriarch, must exert pressure on his Beatitude Deodoros I and his Synod to immediately stop any further sale or lease of church property.

2 - The eventual consecration of an indigenous Patriarch and hierarchs to spearhead the revival of our Orthodox Christian witness in the Holy Land.

3 - The dispatch of Orthodox Christian priests and missionaries from North America to Jordan and the Holy Land to evangelize and initiate a spiritual revival among the faithful.

4 - The initiation of pastoral educational programs for existing clergy and scholarships for seminarians.

5 - The reopening and establishment of new Orthodox schools throughout the Patriarchate of Jerusalem as well as the creation of a Board of Education that can draw on the skills available in the local community.

6 - That the means be provided for the indigenous people to create affordable housing and generate income-producing jobs using the vast real estate holdings and the financial resources of the Patriarchate.

Following this first international meeting, the Task Force started to implement its resolutions through the establishment of chapters across United States, Canada, South America and the Middle East.

By including in its ranks concerned Orthodox Christians from different backgrounds, the Task Force strives to educate in the oldest Church on earth the clergy and the laity of the Holy Land. The Task Force also seeks to help their brothers and sisters in the Patriarchate of Jerusalem spiritually and financially. It also provides literature to awaken Orthodox Christians throughout the world, raising the alarm about the catastrophic situation in the home of our Lord Jesus Christ.

Among its great commitments to this cause, the Task Force took upon itself to publish this historic book in English, which was first published in Beirut in 1893 under the pseudonym of Sheikh 'Abd-el-Ahad-Eshshafi. The Task Force wanted to make this valuable record available to those attending the 2nd Annual International Task Force to be held in Chicago on May 2-5, 1996.

In this dauntless book, the author, then an Archimandrite, described the presence of those monks of the Brotherhood in Lebanon, Syria, Jordan and Palestine as a yoke around the shoulders of the Christians of Antioch and Jerusalem. This courageous fighter was Raphael Hawaweeny of thrice-blessed memory. Before becoming bishop of Brooklyn, he kindled the struggle in the Church of Antioch, writing against the same situation a hundred years ago which prevails today, in Jerusalem.

He repeatedly assured his readers that he would persevere in fighting against the situation and would use all the power given to him to restore indigenous clergy and laity to the See of Antioch. After a long struggle, his efforts finally bore fruit.

In various places, such as Constantinople, Syria, Russia and the United States, Raphael publicized the situation of the Orthodox Christians in Antioch under the control of the Brotherhood in books, bulletins and newspapers. He demonstrated that their domination conflicted with Canon Law and standard Orthodox ecclesiology. He launched his attack by describing the deeds of the Brotherhood which stood in opposition to Orthodox Christian practice.

Raphael never fell into despair, but resisted all attempts to suppress his undertakings. As an Archimandrite, he refused to acknowledge the election of Spyridon as Patriarch of Antioch, calling him "the simoniac" because Spyridon offered the notables of Damascus 10,000 lira for his election.[1]

On account of his opposition, Spyridon inflicted upon Raphael appropriate ecclesiastical punishment, causing him to relinquish his position as head of the Antiochian Metochion in Moscow. Nevertheless, he continued to publish articles in the Russian press in defense of the Antiochian cause.

Then, after being released from the jurisdiction of the Patriarchate of Antioch, he was forced to join the Patriarchate of Moscow. However, he continued writing letters on the issue to people in Damascus and Beirut and certain Antiochian Metropolitans. Raphael was

---

[1] *Many Arabs, like Raphael, also opposed the election of Spyridon because they firmly believed that he would bring no improvement and no benefit.*

the one who inspired some Russians to found the Russian Orthodox Palestine Society,[2] as well as establish schools throughout the Middle East.

Although a multi-cultural person, Raphael was mainly a Philhelenist.[3] He studied in Chalki near Constantinople becoming a lover of the Greek language, theology and culture. What appears to be a Greek antipathy in his writing is, therefore, misleading. He was merely describing historical facts and speaking about the domination over Antioch and Jerusalem by a few monks who happened to be Greek. For this reason he stated the following: "The reader should not imagine that the intention of the Brotherhood is to serve Hellenism in Jerusalem and Palestine. God forbid! If its intention was to serve Hellenism, it would have been using, from its inception until now, all material means to promote Greek education by establishing schools and other centers of education for instructing the indigenous youth, not only in Palestine, but in Syria and Egypt as well."

Having a profound understanding of the history of Christianity, he called those who lived

---

[2] *The Russian Orthodox Palestine Society came into existence on May 21, 1882. The purpose of this organization was to promote knowledge and interest in the holy places.*

[3] *A philhelenist is the one who loves Greek culture.*

under Constantinople Romans, and not Greeks. He said: "The kings of Constantinople were Romans and not Greeks."

He also recounts the story of Omar bin El-Khattab who asked the Patriarch of Jerusalem, Sophronius "What is the name of your branch of Christianity?" Sophronius said that they are called "the Royal People, or the Kingly People, Melkites." However, the name Royal People became forgotten in Syria and Palestine until the beginning of the eighteenth century when certain Orthodox groups became separated from the Orthodox Church in Syria and Lebanon, and became united with Rome, using the name Melkites, i.e., the Royal People.

This book is an expression of a situation still applicable to our own day. Over a hundred years have passed, but Jerusalem today is nevertheless in nearly the same predicament.

Knowing that the courageous efforts of Raphael himself were not immediately crowned with success, the Task Force is aware that it might still take decades of struggle to rejuvenate the Church of Jerusalem.

As Raphael induced the Antiochians to arise "from sleep," the Task Force is redoubling its efforts to lift the yoke from the shoulders of their brothers and sisters in Jerusalem, Palestine and Jordan.

Jesus gave his life for the Church so that Body of Christ might be without spot or wrinkle--so, indeed, the Church might be holy and without blemish. Those who have in their hearts the mission of keeping the Church without blemish have a real interest in the realm of Eastern Orthodox spirituality and the welfare of those believers who have kept the Faith throughout two millennia.

V. Rev. Michel Najim<br>Palm Sunday, 1996

# INTRODUCTION[4]

Giving thanks to God, the Holy One and Provider of all good things, asking Him to lead us in the right way and to guide us to arrive at the correct conclusion, we say that the Brotherhood of the Holy Sepulcher is a strange phenomenon in the history of the Orthodox Church, even in the history of all Christian churches. We have described it as a Greek Brotherhood because it is constituted of only Greek members who are from a foreign land and speak a foreign language. For three and half centuries they have embezzled, through their craftiness and deception, the spiritual and administrative authority in the Patriarchal See of Jerusalem from the hands of the indigenous people, and restricted it to themselves alone, so that the Church of Jerusalem has lost its legal independence and its canonical freedom, and it remains autocephalous in name only. Because the necessary bond between the shepherds and

---

[4] *This valuable historical book was rediscovered in 1995 in Jerusalem. The present translation is missing one Chapter from the original Arabic text which deals with the history of the Brotherhood in the Patriarchate of Antioch.*

the flock, which exists in every autocephalous church, has been broken; it became divided into two segments:

1- The Celibate Greek clergy, who came from a foreign land and who speak a foreign language, as well as their descendants, who have gained power over all the earnings of the Holy Sepulcher and the rest of the Holy Places in Jerusalem and Palestine.

2- The indigenous Orthodox people, who not only were prevented from entering the monastic order, but whose religious and ecclesiastical needs were actually neglected.

The emergence of this Brotherhood in the Orthodox Church is no less strange than the emergence of the Jesuit Brotherhood in the Papal Church. The stranger thing, however, is the simultaneous establishing of these two Brotherhoods, as well as the ways which they used to reach their goals. Just as the Jesuit Brotherhood was established in 1534 at the hands of the Spanish monk Ignatius Loyola, so the Brotherhood of the Holy Sepulcher was established in the same year at the hands of the monk Germanus the Peloponnesian. Both of them adopted a principle contradictory to the spirit of religion and humanity so that they might achieve their ambition, in other words the end justifies the means. In spite of the congruity in the date of establishment and in certain usages, whether lawful or unlawful, to reach their goal, they entertain different views in two areas which give the Jesuits preference from a religious and human standpoint over the monks of Jerusalem. For the goal of the Jesuit Brotherhood was to advocate Papal supremacy for the sake of the glory of the most high God; a goal that does not preclude any one of all the nations under the jurisdiction of the Pope from becoming a member in this Brotherhood. The Brotherhood of the Holy Sepulcher, however, has only one objective--their self-interest covered under the pretext of Greek nationality. For this reason, it does not accept in its membership anyone who is not Greek.

What helped the founders of this Brotherhood to appropriate the spiritual authority of the Church of Jerusalem from the indigenous people, and to restrict it to its own members, was the great influence of the monks of Constantinople who belonged to the same race. Their influence was also due to their closeness to the Sublime Porte. After eliminating the autocephalicity of the Serbian and the Bulgarian Churches through their enormous prerogatives and their wide spiritual authority which had been granted to them by the late Sultan Mahmmed, the conqueror over all the Orthodox people living within the boundaries of the Ottoman Empire. The monks of Al-Phanar,[5] who were at that time the leaders of reviving Greek nationalism, started helping in every way possible their compatriots, i.e., the monks of Jerusalem, to fulfill their national ambition. Their intent was to abduct the spiritual authority of the Church of Jerusalem from the hands of her indigenous children, coveting the tremendous incomes of the Holy Sepulcher. Through these incomes, the monks of Jerusalem have procured the abduction of the Patriarchal See of Jerusalem, making it a hereditary position to be awarded to a successor in conformity with the will of his predecessor. This took place until the time of Cyril the Patriarch of Jerusalem, when they repealed the tradition of inheritance, and started to appoint the Patriarch by an election restricted to the Greeks. The fact is that the indigenous Orthodox element declined in force to such a degree that it was deprived of any will to challenge the issue of the Patriarchal election. When Greece was liberated from the control of the Ottoman Empire through the revolution, the leaders of Greek nationalism moved from Al-Phanar to Athens. However, when the Brotherhood of the Holy Sepulcher, with the aid of Al-Phanar monks, had achieved its objective in the Church of Jerusalem--in such a manner that it maintained only few

---

[5] *El-Phanar is a district in Constantinople where the Ecumenical Patriarch resides, Editor.*

Orthodox indigenous members--it pledged to fulfill the same objective in the neighboring Church of Antioch by leaning on the support of the Greek government through its agents in Syria. Unfortunately, since the children of the Antiochian Church did not at first pay any attention to the abominable intent of the Brotherhood, it was able within a short time to somehow reach its goal. It enthroned the following three members on the Patriarchal See of Antioch: Irotheos, Garasimus and the present Patriarch Spirydon. Moreover, it did not spare any effort to, by any means available, replace all the indigenous bishops of the Church of Antioch with Greek bishops. The time came that when all the Antiochian bishops would come from the Brotherhood, thus easily excluding all the indigenous clergy from ecclesiastical offices. This further prevented them from entering a monastic order, as it had already done to the indigenous Orthodox people in Jerusalem.

We would not have tried to disclose the secret of the Brotherhood of Jerusalem and to reveal its deeds--which are contradictory to the spirit of religion and humanity--were it not for its recent ravenous attack upon the Antiochian Church. In order to procure domination over them, it makes light of the Ordinances and disdains the Laws. In such a situation it is our religious and law-abiding duty to reveal the hidden and the concealed things about the origin and the source of the Brotherhood. We must remove the veil from its deeds, plans, incomes and ambitions, by relying on the earnest historians and devout writers of Greek, Arab, and Russian nationalities, so that we can serve our fellow citizens and our fellow believers. We must also awaken those who are unmindful and those who, because of blind-heartedness or imprudent-mindedness, are coveting to obtain unjust earnings. They failed to recognize that they bring shame upon themselves and upon their fellow citizens and their fellow believers.

# THE ESTABLISHMENT OF THE BROTHERHOOD OF THE HOLY SEPULCHER

All preceding and succeeding historians, even those who were members of the Brotherhood of the Holy Sepulcher, testify that until the year 1534 all the clergy of the Church of Jerusalem, whether they were Patriarchs, bishops, priests or hieromonks, were from the indigenous people of Jerusalem and Palestine. Patriarch Dosytheos, a member of the abovementioned Brotherhood, states in his twelve-volume book *The History of the Patriarchs of Jerusalem,* that, "Since the authority over Jerusalem was in the hands of the Egyptian Sultans, the Patriarchs of Jerusalem were not Greeks, but Arabs. From that time, the dominion of the indigenous people became strong in ecclesiastical issues." Things have followed this pattern until the year 1534, "when Germanus the Peloponysian became the Patriarch of Jerusalem."[1] Constantius I, Patriarch of Constantinople, gives the same testimony saying: "following the defeat of the Latins [the Crusaders] in Jerusalem and up

---

[1] *V., 11, ch., 9, Num., 1, and V. 11 ch., 7, Num., 2.*

until the year 1534, all the Jerusalemite Patriarchs were Arabs, nominated and elected from the hierarchies of the See of Jerusalem, from the indigenous Arab Orthodox clergy."[2] The renowned Greek scholar Alexander Epsilanidis says in his book, *Following the Conquest of Constantinople,* that all the Jerusalemite Patriarchs till the above-mentioned Germanus were "from the Arabs and from the indigenous inhabitants of Palestine." Thus it is clear that the administration of the Jerusalemite Patriarchate until Patriarch Germanus was in the hands of the indigenous Orthodox clergy.

While the indigenous Patriarchs of Jerusalem were holding fast to the right teaching of the Orthodox Church by not discriminating among Arabs, Greeks, Georgians, and Bulgarians, that is, by accepting into the clerical order anyone who desired to embrace the monastic life regardless of his nationality, provided that he was an Orthodox Christian, the above-mentioned Germanus, being fraught with the spirit of Greek Nationalism--which is contradictory to the spirit of Orthodox faith and of Christian religion--as soon as he ascended the Patriarchal See of Jerusalem, proscribed the indigenous Orthodox clergy from all high ecclesiastical orders, and

---

[2] *See the edicts of this Patriarch, printed in Constantinople, in 1866, page 231.*

restricting them to his countrymen. The great Russian historian Andrew Morafiov states: "Even though a Greek, Germanus mixed with the Arabs to such a degree that there was no suspicion that he was not an Arab. Eventually, he reached the level of Hierarch. And when he finally was elevated to Patriarch of Jerusalem, an office held by him for over thirty years,[3] he substituted at the death of each Arab bishop a Greek bishop, so that during his long-term period all the bishops became Greek. Then he passed a Law which is observed until now that a non Greek person cannot be elevated to the level of bishop."[4] He was not completely satisfied with the Hellenization of the hierarchy, but even attempted to have a Greek successor. Thus, according to the account of Patriarch Dositheos, "when Patriarch Germanus was visiting Constantinople, he found in the Church of Saint Nicholas, located outside the walls of the city in a place called Iakbo, a Peloponysian priest, i.e., his compatriot. He took the priest with him to Jerusalem and tonsured him a monk, and made him his successor before his

---

[3] *His Patriarchate lasted for 45 years: from 1534 until 1579, Dosytheos, V. 11 Ch., 7, Num., 4.*

[4] *Relations of Russia with the East, Volume one, 56-57.*

death."[5] How did he manage to make this priest his successor? Relying on the minutes of Germanus resignation and the election of Sophronius (the name of that priest), which were kept in Arabic and translated by Dosytheos into Greek, listen to what patriarch Dosytheos says: "In 7087 [to Adam=1579 A.D.] on Tuesday Patriarch Germanus called to his cell all the Jerusalemite leaders of the people, together with clergy, both old and young, saying: 'My children, may God bless you! I cannot live any more in the patriarchate, for I am now of old age. So elect another Patriarch to take my place.' Accepting his words, they all called Sylvestros, Patriarch of Alexandria, to the cell, where already were present Metropolitans Rorothaos and Nectarios, and Bishops Eugenios of Sinai, and Simon of Holy Anna of Damascus. According to his will, all of them, i.e., the Patriarch of Alexandria, the Metropolitans, and the bishops, agreed to elect a successor to Germanus. They nominated three candidates, and presented the names to the Patriarch of Alexandria. On the second day, the Patriarch of Alexandria and all the bishops placed the ballots on the Holy table, and celebrated the Divine Liturgy. After the Liturgy they brought a child to the altar to choose by lot one name. He went in and drew the ballot

---

[5] *V., 11. Ch., 7, Num., 3.*

of the priest Sophronius."⁶ However, in the narrative of Dosytheos there are several ambiguous things:

1-Why did Germanus call a non-Jerusalemite Patriarch for the election? Does not this procedure show that Germanus was cautious so as not to provoke any antagonism from the indigenous Church? He may have made a secret agreement with the Patriarch of Alexandria to help attain his goal, i.e., to appoint Sophronios as his successor.

2-Why did Dosytheos not mention the names of the three candidates written on the ballots? Does this not make the reader suspicious about the possibility that the name of Sophronius was written on all three ballots?

3-Why did the Patriarch of Jerusalem keep the ballots for the second day, and not bring them to the Church on the same day? Do not these actions show that the Patriarch of Alexandria may have changed the ballots in accordance with the will of Germanus, thus making the three of them have the name of Sophronios?

4 - Why was there a need to use the child to select one of the three ballots--an

---

⁶ *V. 11, Ch. 7, Num. 4.*

action which does not exist in the history of the Orthodox Church or in the history of any other Christian church--had it not been the will of Germanus and his supporters to deceive the pure hearts of the indigenous people?

Whatever the case may be, Germanos succeeded in making his compatriot Sophronios his successor. When Sophronius was enthroned, he followed his predecessor's example in ordaining only Greeks to the monastic order. After twenty nine years of his patriarchate, Sophronios relinquished his position due to his advanced age and the enormous debts which he accumulated, debts totaling nearly twelve-thousand golden pounds. This was occurred from his dispute with the Latins regarding the Holy Places. He then appointed his countryman, Theophanis, and sent him abroad to collect alms.[7]

Following in the steps of his predecessors, Theophanis did not ordain any clergy in Jerusalem and Palestine, except his compatriots, and especially his relatives. He ordained his cousin, Athanasios, as the Metropolitan of Bethlehem, and his kinsman, Paysios, as an abbot of Galta Monastery in Yash. His patriarchate of thirty seven years, was spent mainly in traveling and collecting funds.

---

[7] *Dosytheos, V., 11, ch., 7., Nm., 6.*

When he passed away in Constantinople, in the Jerusalemite Metochion [dependency] which he had built for himself, he was succeeded by his kinsman Paces in the year 1645.[8]

However, the abduction of the spiritual authority in the Church of Jerusalem and its restriction to a minority of foreign places and of a foreign language, united by their nationality and their family relationship, attracted the attention of the local Orthodox and the rest of the Greeks, primarily the monks of Al-Phanar. And so after the death of Patriarch Theophanis in Constantinople, the Ecumenical Patriarch Parthenios, longing to affiliate the Church of Jerusalem to the Church of Constantinople, nominated one of his bishops, Ioannikos, as Metropolitan of Pyria, to be the Patriarch of Jerusalem. However, he did not succeed in his endeavor because the monks of Jerusalem had all the wealth. Concerning this, Patriarch Dosytheos says the following:

"Upon the death of Theophanis, it occurred to the Ecumenical Patriarch's[9] mind--a self-conceited man--to ordain Metropolitan Pyria Ioannikos as Patriarch of Jerusalem. Knowing that the Patriarchate of Jerusalem is

---

[8] *Dosethaous, V., 12, ch., 1., Nm., 10.*

[9] *-Parthenios*

in need of a sincere and amiable Patriarch and a leader, not a despot, the Jerusalemites, i.e., the monks of Jerusalem who lived in the monasteries of the Holy Sepulcher in Moldavia, embarked upon propitiating Basil, prince of Moldavia, an affluent and powerful man, to nominate Paces as abbot of Galta monastery. Prince Basil wrote to the Patriarch of Constantinople and the Synod informing them of the nomination of Paysios by the monks of Jerusalem. The Patriarch of Constantinople, because he feared Prince Basil, did not dare repudiate the nomination of Paces, instead he sent to Yash the Metropolitan of Larissa, the Exarch Gregory, accompanied by hierarchical attendants to enthrone Paces as Patriarch of Jerusalem."[10]

As the Patriarch of Constantinople, Parthenios, did not succeed in subjugating the Church of Jerusalem to his authority, the indigenous children of the Jerusalem Patriarchate did not get their wish to be rid of the yoke of the Greek monks of Jerusalem. Following Paysios enthronement as Patriarch, he was determined to travel by land to Jerusalem. Since he feared the resistance of the people and the clergy of Jerusalem, he took along with him "a Sultanic man," i.e., a royal

---

[10] *Dosytheos, V., 12, ch., 1., Nm., 10.*

official of Constantinople, to try to force the people to recognize him. Dosytheos states,

"The Synod and the fathers of Jerusalem accepted him as one of their own, and acknowledged him as a canonical Patriarch--for they were compatriots and relatives--but the clergy--the majority of the priests and ascetics were still indigenous--opposed him. Then the clergy and laity went beyond the walls of the Holy City and made a pile of stones to resist the Patriarch. But being a courageous person, Paysios talked secretly to the local authorities and gave them some money so that they would not allow anyone to be disrespectful to him. Then, afterwards, he filed suit against the indigenous Christians. The suit, greatly intimidating them, led to their castigation. From that time on, they were peaceful, living calmly and with the fear of God."[11]

He concluded his statement saying, "This is the first good thing Paysios did in Jerusalem."[12]

My native readers, you may talk without any embarrassment about the hardships of the indigenous Orthodox people of Jerusalem, such

---

[11] *V., 12, Ch. 2, Nm., 1.*

[12] *Ibid.*

as imprisonment, banishment, extermination, affliction, persecution and tribulation at the hand of Paces who was called to be their Father, Pastor and Patriarch.

In order to learn about the audacity of Patriarch Pasyios, listen to what Dosytheos narrated in his book. "Once, when Pasyios was passing through the village of Panagia next to Toborotchi in Moldavia, burglars suddenly came upon him. He defended himself and was victorious over twelve of them and seized their horses."[13] No wonder, that this highhanded Paysios did not fear God when he bribed the governors in Constantinople to banish his enemy, Parthenios, the Patriarch of Constantinople, and execute him on a stake. Paysios sealed his virtues by enacting a law, which surpassed even the law passed by Germanos, that in the future no indigenous Orthodox would be accepted, not only to the bishopric, but to any clerical or monastic order- - even a reader or an attendant in a monastery! By this law, which contradicts Canon Law as well as the spirit of religion and humanity, Paysios cut off the final attachment of the pastors and their flock in the Church of Jerusalem.

---

[13] *V., 12, Ch. 1, Nm., 10.*

Nevertheless, the Just and Omnipotent God permitted Paysios, after he lost his law-suit against the Armenians and the Latins regarding the monastery of Saint James, was imprisoned and tortured in Constantinople. But after paying a great amount of money, he was set free. However, on his way back, he had a repugnant death on a ship near the seashore of Castia Orison. He was buried in a deserted place where he was profaned by Metropolitan of Lydda and Prochoros, but he was lamented by the passengers.[14]

Upon the death of Paysios in 1662, those Jerusalem monks who dwell in the Jerusalemite Metochion in Constantinople were able, with the help of the above-mentioned Prince Basil and with the consent of the Constantinopolitan Synod, to elect Nektarios as Patriarch of Jerusalem. After seven years Nektarios decided to resign from the Patriarchate for three reasons:

-His chronic illness.

-The annoyance and harassment from the monks of Jerusalem because he was not elected by them.

---

[14] *Dosytheos, V., 12. Ch.,2, Nm., 1.*

-The accumulation of debts at the Patriarchate because of the squabble between the Greeks, on the one side, and the Armenians and the Franciscans on the other, with regard to the Holy Land.

The first one to learn of his resignation was Dosytheos, the writer of, *The History of the Patriarchs of Jerusalem*. He made every effort, according to what he said in his history, to convince Patriarch Nektarios to elect a successor to him, not in Constantinople, but in Jerusalem from the members of the brotherhood, for "the debts and the commotions of the monks of Jerusalem will not be properly resolved, except through electing a patriarch from the monks of Jerusalem."[15] Nektarios, however, did not pay attention to Dosytheos. Rather, he ordered him to head for Larrisa, where the Sultan was visiting, so he could obtain from him an order to elect anyone the Sultan wanted to become the Patriarch of Jerusalem. And so the Sultan elected Dosytheos himself a successor to Nektarios.[16]

In 1669, when Dosytheos was enthroned as Patriarch of Jerusalem, he hastened to reconfirm the law which was legislated by his

---

[15] *V., 12, Ch., 3, Nm., 6.*

[16] *V., 12, Ch., 3, Nm., 6.*

two predecessors, Germanos and Paysios, of not accepting any indigenous person from the Patriarchate to be a member of the Brotherhood. In addition to this he reorganized the Brotherhood writing its constitution and by-laws, where no indigenous person from Jerusalem or Palestine was eligible to become a member of the Brotherhood, and none could be elected as a bishop, a Metropolitan or Patriarch except from among its members. These laws are still in effect until our present day, but it is kept secret; so no one is allowed to know about them, except the members who join pledging allegiance to the Brotherhood.

At first, the intention behind the above-mentioned dictum was to deprive the children of the Church of Jerusalem from the high clerical orders, so that the members of the brotherhood could dominate the Church and the Holy Land. They did not oppose the indigenous Antiochians to join monastic life in one of the monasteries in Jerusalem. Two of whom later were able to become patriarchs in Jerusalem:

1- Sophronios, born in Chales near Allepo, became the Patriarch of Jerusalem in 1771. Then he was transferred to Constantinople in 1774 due to his virtues and education. Constantios, Patriarch of Constantinople, testified that he was a righteous and holy man, well-versed in Arabic, Turkish and Greek. Sophronios was a great preacher, and he was always followed by a great group of people who used to flock from all the neighborhoods of Constantinople to listen to his sermons every Sunday in the great Church.

2- Anthimos, the Antiochian, was enthroned as Patriarch of Jerusalem in 1789. Constantios, Patriarch of Constantinople, testified that he was a Godly man, proficient in theology and well-versed in Arabic, Turkish and Greek. He translated into Arabic some patristic literature, the most important is the book of *Guidance*[17] which is still known among the Arab Christians in Syria, Egypt and Palestine. He died in 1807.

Those two Patriarchs who were the luminaries of their age and the pride of the Patriarchs of Jerusalem were the last two indigenous patriarchs of Jerusalem. Expanding its despotism, the Brotherhood, subsequently prevented any non-Greek person from becoming one of its members.

Thus, we do not deny that the three Greek Patriarchs of Jerusalem, Nektarios, Dositheos and his nephew Chrisanthos, were superior to their Greek predecessors and successors in education and scholarship. They

---

[17] *Al-Hidayat.*

left great writings like the book of Nektarios the *Syntagma*--the Constitution--against the primacy of the Pope of Rome, and the history of the Church of Jerusalem with its patriarchs. There is also the refutations to the innovations of the Roman Catholic Church written by Dositheos, and the introduction to geography written by Chrisanthos.

Being a righteous person in mind and soul, Nektarios' heart refused to follow the steps of his predecessors who were more like ravenous wolves than good shepherds. He saw the fierce resistance of the Jerusalemite monks when he declined to persecute the indigenous Orthodox, and so chose to retire, devoting himself to writing till the end of his life.

His two successors, Dositheos and Chrisanthos, following the steps of their compatriots, Germanus, Sophronius and Paces, outmatched them in supporting the usurpation of spiritual authority in the Church of Jerusalem and in neglecting the indigenous Orthodox. Moreover, they persecuted and oppressed them by reporting them to governors and rulers in an effort to eradicate and wipe them out. In order to freely understand the insincerity of Dositheos, of whom the Brotherhood boasts, by calling him a righteous great and holy man, the guileless pastor,[18] hear how he explains in his history the abduction of spiritual authority from the indigenous children of the Church, saying,

"Since the authority over Jerusalem was in the hands of the Egyptian Sultans, the Patriarchs of Jerusalem were not Greeks, but Arabs. From that time on, the dominion of the indigenous people became strong in ecclesiastical issues. But since the Arabs were a despicable people, who looked after their special interests more than their duty, the Arab patriarchs, together with their relatives and compatriots, used to run haphazardly the Patriarchate.

Because the Patriarchs became engaged in disputes with Armenian and Latins regarding the Holy Places, they let the Arabs follow the old tradition of being in charge of the income of the Patriarchate. The indigenous Arabs did not consider anything except their personal interests."[19]

Dosytheos failed to understand that by these insulting statements about the Arabs, and

---

[18] *In the Greek magazine "ΣΩΤΗΡ" of 1892, there is an article written about the Patriarch Dosytheos by Archimandrite Cyril Athanasiades.*

[19]-*(V., 12, CH., 2, Nm., 1)*

especially about their patriarchs, he contradicted himself because he himself tells us that most of the Greek Patriarchs from Germanos to Chrisanthos were not only compatriots, but relatives and kindred. They simply did not elevate anyone to high positions except their relatives. Dosytheos himself elevated his nephew Chrisanthos to be the Metropolitan of Ceasarea and then made him his successor. In a previous chapter, he exalted the Arab Patriarchs with strong arguments which refute his unjust dispraise. Listen to what he said,

"Since Palestine was under the Egyptian Sultans, and since the Greeks were under the Ottoman authority, it was not easy for the Christians to visit the Holy Land. For this reason, the Arab Patriarchs were extremely indigent. The proof of this is that:

1-The monasteries and the Holy Sepulcher and the Church of Bethlehem were not maintained, and some of its sections were about to collapse.

2-The Arab Patriarchs had neither church supplies nor appropriate vestments, rather they used to celebrate the Liturgy with vestments made out of yarn and calico. The Trikeron was made out of cast iron.

3-The Arab Patriarchs earned their living from the work of their hands like the Apostle Paul; they had no income and no gratuity."[20]

If the Arab Patriarchs under these difficult circumstances "earned their living from the work of their hands like the Apostle Paul; they had no income and no gratuity," where is the great income Dosytheos mentioned, supposedly being distributed among their relatives and their compatriots? Isn't the statement of Dosytheos a great libel against those holy men, the successors of the Apostles, who also did not have any income or gratuity, but maintained the flock of the Orthodox Church and faithfully preserved the Holy Places?

My native reader, this is the way which the unprecedented Brotherhood of the Holy Sepulcher was established, with its principles and intentions which are contradictory to the spirit of religion and humanity, as well as to the teachings of the Apostle Paul who said that in the Church of Christ, "There is no Greek and Jew, circumscribed or uncircumscribed,

---

[20] *V., 11, Ch., 7, Nm., 2.*

barbarian, Scythian, slave and free, but Christ is all in all!"[21]

---

[21] *Col. 3:11.*

## THE BROTHERHOOD OF THE HOLY SEPULCHER AND THE HOLY LAND

By studying properly Church History from the beginning of the Christian era till the time of the abduction of Church of Jerusalem at the hands of Germanus and his successors, we learned that all the Holy Places in Jerusalem and Palestine, such as monasteries, churches and shrines, were in the hands of the indigenous Orthodox people of Jerusalem and Palestine by virtue of their native Patriarchs. Those righteous Patriarchs sacrificed themselves and shed their blood for the sake of preserving the Holy Sepulcher and all the Holy Places. Thus, when the Arabs captured Jerusalem and Palestine in 637 under the leadership of the Caliph Omar Ibn Al-khatab, the Jerusalemite Patriarch Sophronios with his clergy hastened to welcome him, giving him the keys of the Church of the Resurrection as a sign of compliance and submission. Delighted at Patriarch Sophronios, the Caliph gave him a document of guardianship, confirming to him and to his people the right of predominance over the Holy Places and of leadership over the non-Orthodox people living in Jerusalem, like the Iberians, the Ethiopians, the pilgrims from all nationalities, the Franks, Copts, Armenians, Nestorians, Jacobites and Maronites. This Arabic document of guardianship is still preserved in the office of the Jerusalemite Metochion in Constantinople.

There is a local tradition which says that when the Caliph Omar Ibn El-Khatab wanted to write the document of guardianship to Patriarch Sophronios, after he had heard that Christians were divided into different groups such as Jacobites, Nestorians, Armenians, Maronites and so forth, he asked him: "What is the name of your branch of Christianity?" Sophronios entreated him to give him sometime, so that he could find a good name pleasing to the Caliph. While he was absorbed in praying fervently, he was inspired to call his people by the first word he would hear in the service. Then listening attentively, he heard the deacon reading the fifth Psalm from the first hour: "O my King and my Lord." Then he knew that he should call his people "the Royal People, or the Kingly People." Upon finishing his prayer he told the Caliph that they should be called "Royal People," "Melkites." The Caliph approved this name and named Sophronios in the document: "The Patriarch of the Royal People." **From that time till the end of the Arabic period, the Orthodox of Palestine and Syria came to be called the Royal People.**

When the power transferred to the Ottomans they called the Rum Orthodox Christians or Romans, even the Orthodox emperors of Constantinople were known by the Muslims as the Roman Emperors or the Rum Emperors-- The kings of Constantinople were Romans and not Greeks.

The name Royal People became forgotten in Syria and Palestine until the beginning of this century[22] when the Catholics, who separated themselves from the Orthodox Church in Syria and created their own Church, arrogated to themselves the name Melkites, i.e., the Royal People.

Whatever the case may be, it is right to say that Omar bin El-Khattab called the Patriarch of Jerusalem and his people by the name: "The Royal Nation" to discern them from non-Orthodox people.

In order to advocate their false claim to control of the Holy Sepulcher and the other Holy Places, the members of the Holy Sepulcher started to claim that the document of guardianship was given by Caliph Omar to the Greek nation, because the Patriarch Sophronios and his people were Greeks. Thus the Caliph called them "The Royal Nation." But what

---

[22] *That is the 18th Century, Editor.*

disclaims the allegation of the Greeks is the above-mentioned local tradition. Even if we presuppose the fallacy of this tradition we cannot concede with their allegation that the "royal nation" is the Greek Nation,

-First, because there was no Greek Empire at that time, but a Roman Empire, and the inhabitants of that Empire were called, and called themselves, Romans, and not Greeks.

-Second, if Patriarch Sophronios and his people were genuine Greeks, he would have called them "the Greek nation," and there would be no need to have a new name, i.e., the"Royal Nation."

-Third, suppose that Sophronios and his people were Greeks, and that the Royal document of guardianship was given to the Greeks, this does not justify the abduction of authority over the Holy Sepulcher and the Holy Land, for they were strangers to the land. Only the indigenous people possess the right to have legal authority over Jerusalem. Historically, we know that none of the Arab Muslims became Christian. On the contrary, many Christians embraced Islam. Thus, the Orthodox people who survived until our age in both Jerusalem and Palestine are the descendants of the native Orthodox people who lived there during the time of Caliph Omar bin El-Khattab and Patriarch Sophronios. Their Arabic language does not deprive them of the right to manage what was confirmed by Caliph Omar Bin El-Khattab to their ancestors. There is no prudent person who would say that the Orthodox people of Asia Minor are strangers because they speak Turkish, for none of the Turks became Christian. On the contrary, many Greek Christians of Asia Minor also embraced Islam.

When the Crusaders occupied Jerusalem in 1099, they appropriated the Holy Sepulcher and parts of the Holy Places until Youssef Salah El-Dein, the Sultan of Egypt, threw them out of Jerusalem. He reconfirmed the document of guardianship by Omar Bin El-Khattab and returned the Holy Sepulcher and the Holy Places to the native Orthodox people, who, after a short time following the Arab occupation, started to be called Arabs, because of the widespread use of the Arabic language in Palestine and Syria. Five years later, the Crusaders re-occupied Jerusalem, but, again after a short time, the Ayyubid Sultan of Egypt threw them out of Jerusalem and "returned the Holy Sepulcher and the Holy Land to the indigenous Orthodox Arab people."[23] When the Mamluks triumphed over the Ayyubids in 1250, the fourth Mamluk Sultan, El-Zaher, was able to force the Crusaders out of Jerusalem. He rebuilt the walls of Jerusalem and secured the

---

[23] *See Constantinides, page 230.*

right of the indigenous Orthodox people over the Holy Places. After the abatement of the Mamluks' kingdom and the emergence of the Circassians,[24] from 1389 until the Ottoman period, the Holy Places remained in the hands of the indigenous Orthodox people, for each Sultan issued at his enthronement a directive confirming the document of guardianship of Omar Bin El-Khattab.

During the Mamluks' kingdom, some Latin religious, Franciscans, having no place to accommodate them, requested lodging from Joachim, Patriarch of Jerusalem. Following the Christian duty of love, he gave them the monastery of Zion located outside Jerusalem. In doing so, he alienated the indigenous Moslems, who appropriated the monastery from the Franciscans and converted it to a mosque. The Franciscans came back requesting fervently from Patriarch Joachim to allow them to use another monastery in return for rent. He gave them the monastery of Saint John the Theologian inside Jerusalem, and gave the monastery of Saint James to the Armenians. This is what the Arab patriarchs permitted to be given to Latin and Armenians pilgrims, done in conformity with the spirit of Christian love, and not out of weakness nor mismanagement,

---

[24]-*Or the Cherkess.*

as the monks of Jerusalem are now unjustly accusing them.

When Muhammed II conquered Constantinople in 1453, the Patriarch of Jerusalem, Athanasios III, came to Constantinople and obtained from him a directive confirming the document of guardianship of Omar Bin El-Khattab, dated the half of the month Shaoual,[25] 862 years after the Hegira. Afterwards, when Sultan Saleem I conquered Jerusalem, Patriarch Atallah, the last indigenous Patriarch, together with some clergy and representatives of the people, hastened to Constantinople where he appeared before the Sultan. Giving him the document of guardianship of Omar Bin El-Khattab and all the above-mentioned Sultanic directives, he requested that he confirm them with a new directive. Delighted at the attitude, intelligence and simplicity of Patriarch Atallah, he gave him a directive dated on the 25th of Sofr,[26] the year 923 after the Hegira. After the death of Sultan Saleem I and the enthronement of Sultan Soulaiman, Patriarch Atallah went again to Constantinople and obtained a new directive, confirming all the previous ones.

---

[25] Then month of the festival of the breaking of the Islamic fast. It is the tenth month of the Lunar year.

[26] The second month of the Arabian calendar.

Thus, the indigenous Patriarchs of Jerusalem spared no effort to maintain the Holy Sepulcher and all the Holy Places. And so during their times none of the non-Orthodox churches dared to claim any authority over them, for all of the people knew and recognized that the authority over the Holy Places belonged to the indigenous Orthodox people of Jerusalem and Palestine. This authority was acknowledged by the victorious Ottoman Sultans. After the abduction of Patriarchal authority during the reign of Mourad IV, when the Latins claimed the authority of the Manger of Bethlehem based upon a forged firman, Patriarch Theophanes was unable to prove the right of the Orthodox people until he summoned the indigenous Oikonomos of the Patriarchate of Jerusalem, Father Hanna, who proved in eloquent Arabic in the presence of the Great Vizier, the Muslim sheik, and some military officials, the right of the Orthodox people and the invalidity of the Latin case. Then he obtained a Sultanic directive in favor of Patriarch Theophanes dated on the middle of the first Jumada 1047 after the Hegira.

Following the death of Patriarch Atallah thrice-blessed memory, the Patriarch Germanus succeeded him and started to replace all the indigenous bishops with Greek bishops. Then the non-Orthodox people saw that the Holy Places were embezzled from the hands of their legal guardians and placed under the authority of a group who spoke a strange language and were from a strange place. And so based upon that fact that the Greeks have no better rights over the Holy Sepulcher and the Holy Places than anybody else, all the non-Orthodox churches rushed to claim the right to have authority over the Holy Places. Thus, the disputes and conflicts started between the monks of Jerusalem and the non-Orthodox churches. In spite of all the money paid by the monks of Jerusalem to protect the Holy Places, they failed to protect them like the legal indigenous Orthodox guardians. Sometime after the abduction of the Holy Places by the monks of Jerusalem, the Latins seized some, the Armenians took others, and other churches took possession of still others. These disputes are still in full swing, and will never cease so long as the Greek monks of Jerusalem continue to control the Jerusalemite church and are domineering the Holy Sepulcher and all the Holy Places contrary to every canon and law.

What supports the above charge is that the non-Orthodox people considered the Greek monks, from Germanos until now, foreign usurpers. This opinion was expressed by many Latins, and especially by the French writer Eugene Bori in his book, "*The Holy Land*," where he called the Greek monks not only foreigners but "embezzlers aiming at dominating the three patriarchal Sees:

Jerusalem, Antioch and Alexandria."[27] Patriarch Constantios makes every effort to disprove the book of Eugene Bori, endeavoring to prove that the Orthodox people of Jerusalem and Palestine with their Patriarchs and clergy were from the beginning Greeks. Consequently the monks of the Brotherhood of Jerusalem are not foreigners or embezzlers. Yet the true history, according to the above-mentioned testimony of Constantios himself and of Patriarch Dosytheos, affirms that the authority of the Church of Jerusalem and all the Holy Places from the beginning of Christianity until Germanos, the Peloponnesian, in 1534 was in the hands of the indigenous Orthodox people of Jerusalem and Palestine. So there is no doubt that the monks of Jerusalem are foreign embezzlers:

First, they have formed a Brotherhood whose membership is limited to Greeks, with the exclusion of all other Orthodox Christians, especially the indigenous children of the Church of Jerusalem.

Second, they invented in the great litany the tradition of commemorating all the departed Patriarchs of Jerusalem--say the chairmen of the Brotherhood--from Germanos to the newly departed Irotheos (predecessor of Nikodemos). This act shows clearly that the

---

[27] *See the provisions of Constantios, page 251-268.*

Brotherhood is a foreign organization, for it commemorates the succession of the Patriarchs beginning only with Germanos. At least if it mentioned another Patriarch of Jerusalem who came before Germanus, i.e., Patriarch Atallah, along with the Greek Patriarchs, it would have at least preserved the succession of the authentic Patriarchs of Jerusalem, and it would have kept the right to say that its Patriarchs are the successors of James the Apostle, the first Bishop of Jerusalem. From the other side it would have proved that it is far from the spirit of nationalism, which contradicts the teaching of the Gospel and the Church. What proves our statement is that the Brotherhood did not decide to commemorate the names of the Greek Patriarchs except for nationalistic purposes. Thus, the first Antiochian Patriarch from the Brotherhood, the late Irotheos introduced this tradition to the Antiochian Church. He gave orders to commemorate the names of the Antiochian Patriarchs beginning from Sylvestros, the first Greek Patriarch of Antioch in 1724. His two successors, Garasimos and the present Patriarch Spyridon, confirmed this tradition in the Antiochian Church. Since both of them are members of the Brotherhood of the Holy Sepulcher, they have proved that they do not have any relationship with those who preceded them, from the indigenous Patriarchs who were the successors of the Apostles.

## THE BROTHERHOOD OF THE HOLY SEPULCHER AND THE INCOME OF THE PATRIARCHATE OF JERUSALEM.

One of the reasons that motivated this group to embezzle the spiritual authority of the Church of Jerusalem is their covetousness of the income of the Holy Land, which started to increase a few years before the enthronement of Patriarch Germanos. The reason for this increased income is the peace which prevailed in Palestine, Syria and all the Ottoman countries following the triumph of the victorious Ottoman Sultans over Jerusalem, with the result that Christian pilgrims from all over the world hastened to visit the Holy Land. Thus, since its establishment, the Brotherhood of the Holy Sepulcher used methods to ostracize the indigenous clergy from the hierarchy, planning to direct all the proceeds of the Holy Places into its own hands. So let us trace the voyages of the Greek Patriarchs to collect money in the name of the Holy Sepulcher and to purchase properties which might supply them with the means of affluence and luxury.

Having Greek princes in Moldavia and Serbia, they were able to change the title of ownership of many monasteries together with their properties so that they come under the name of the Holy Sepulcher. But they were not satisfied with just the monasteries, and so they convinced many rich Orthodox people of that land to turn over the title of their best properties to the Holy Sepulcher, in order to protect them from the attacks of the Catholic Slavs. These attacks achieved their desired results by wrenching away those countries from the hands of the Ottoman Empire. Thus, in a short period of time, the monks of Jerusalem were able to obtain many monasteries and vast properties in Moldavia and Serbia. Then, laying their snares in Georgia and the Caucasus, they sought properties and lands from the hands of the indigenous Orthodox people. Their proceeds increased tremendously, and the earnings poured down on them in torrents. Covetousness consumed wholly those monks to such an extent that they were not satisfied with the enormous proceeds of these properties, but they started to build in the main cities buildings called metochia, so that they could collect alms under the name of the Holy Sepulcher.

In particular we should refer to the Metochia in Jerusalem, Constantinople, Moscow, Athens, Tagnerock--Southern Russia--Azmir, Crete, Chalki, and many others in Anatolia, Macedonia and Thraki. All these metochia had properties whose harvests were exploited by the monks of Jerusalem. Leading a luxurious and sumptuous life, they ignored God, and became involved in immorality, especially the abbots in Moldavia. They changed their homes from simple monastic cells to huge mansions which could not be distinguished from the mansions of Princes. They were preoccupied with pomp, splendor, sumptuous food and all manner of indulgence. They reached the highest levels of the autocracy. Noting that the abbots would not go from one place to the other without a special cabriolet, the native people in these countries were deeply disturbed by their actions. When the government of Moldavia saw their atrocious actions, it deported them in 1864, and took possession of all their monasteries together with their properties, changing them into charity homes and military places, with the proceeds of the properties entering into the treasury of the government.[28]

However, there were still many properties remaining under the control of the monks of the Holy Sepulcher in Serbia, because Serbia had come under the authority of Russia

---

[28] *In addition to the Holy Sepulcher properties, there were properties which belonged to the Churches of Constantinople, Alexandria and Antioch administered by the monks of Jerusalem. The last Abbot of the Antiochian monastery was Irotheos, the nephew of Patriarch Irotheos, who became the abbot of Balamand monastery and who died there in 1886.*

in 1812. In addition to these, they had valuable properties in Georgia, Caucasus and many other countries. Their value exceed 6,000,000 Russian riyal, i.e., 9,000,000 piasters. The following is a statement of the income of the Brotherhood as it appeared in the budget of the Patriarchate of Jerusalem in 1890 published by Basil Chitrovou the Secretary of the Palestinian Imperial Orthodox Society.

| Ordinary income | Riyal |
|---|---|
| Properties in Jerusalem. | 64100 |
| Properties in Izmir. | 8900 |
| Pr. , in Crete & Cyprus | 1600 |
| Pr., in Istanbul | 2200 |
| Pr., in Greece | 1500 |
| Pr., in Georgia | 2300 |
| Pr., in Serbia & Russia | 138500 |
| Russian donations | 17500 |
| Donations for schools | 55700 |
| Pilgrims | 110900 |
| Special income | |

| | |
|---|---|
| Pr., in Serbia, 1884 | 23496 |
| Selling papers | 13752 |
| Interest | 6554 |
| From debtors | 621 |
| Loan from Russia | 313165 |
| Loan from a Jewish Bank | 169769 |
| Loan from individuals | 85452 |
| -------- | --------- |
| Total | 1016009 |

Thus, if we overlook the special income exceeding one million Russian riyal, i.e., fifteen million piasters the ordinary yearly income comes close to a half million Russian riyal, i.e., seven million piasters. No one except God himself and the members of the Brotherhood can know the exact amount of the special gifts which come from the pilgrims. In order to know, O reader, the great amounts which the monks of Jerusalem collect from the pilgrims and the benefactors, we need to mention the amount of money which the Patriarchate borrowed from certain members of the Brotherhood during the patriarchate of Nikodimos:

From Seraphim, the Archimandrite of the Holy Sepulcher, one hundred thousands Russian riyal (i.e., 302862 francs); and from his assistant, Archimandrite Euthemios, thirteen thousand riyal (i.e., 40,000 francs). From the Metropolitan of El-Tour, Spyridon (the present Patriarch of Antioch), twenty thousands riyal (76480 francs). The interest given to Seraphim was 7% and the interest given to Euthemios and Spyridon was 8%. If the Archimandrites of the Holy Sepulcher were able to lend the church thousands of riyals, I wonder how much capital each one of them has? And how many thousands do their bishops and Metropolitans have?

Now that you know, my reader, the incredible amount of their annual income, do you still wonder why they adhere to their present position which provides them with such great material income? Do you yet find it strange that they endeavor to weaken and eradicate the indigenous Orthodox, those who have the legal rights over the Holy Places, the sources of all these abundant revenues?

Yet perhaps you wonder why the Brotherhood endeavored to seize the spiritual authority of the Antiochian church, in spite of the fact that the income of the Antiochian Patriarchate is nothing compared to the income of the Patriarchate of Jerusalem.

The aim of the Brotherhood in the Patriarchate of Antioch is not only its income, but to take exclusive control of its indigenous people for the singular purpose of leaving them in the shadow of spiritual, mental, moral and material death. They are afraid that our success under an indigenous Patriarch would draw the attention of their brethren in the Patriarchate of Jerusalem to the appropriation by the monks of Jerusalem of the income from the Holy Places. This would bring misfortune to the monks, because they know that they are strangers, and have no right to take possession of the Holy Land which is the right of the native children of Jerusalem. If the indigenous people were to wake up, they would have the full right to discharge the foreign monks and to recover the properties of their fathers and their forefathers.

# THE BROTHERHOOD OF THE HOLY SEPULCHER AND THE INDIGENOUS CHILDREN OF THE CHURCH OF JERUSALEM

One may ask: What does the Brotherhood accomplish that benefits the indigenous children of church of Jerusalem? After all it abducted from them all spiritual authority and took possession of the income of the Holy Places, which now reach annually the amount of seven million piasters. Before seizing the properties of the Holy Sepulcher in Moldavia, its income was over forty million piasters annually.

To answer the important question raised above, we turn to the words of a great Russian writer who lived in Jerusalem and Palestine for a long time, and became associated with both the monks of Jerusalem and the indigenous children of Jerusalem: "I answer this question objectively saying that the Brotherhood did not do anything for the benefit of the Orthodox of Jerusalem and Palestine, neither morally nor financially. Not even simple churches which are appropriate for worship were built for them. The Brotherhood opened neither a seminary to prepare spiritual servants nor elementary schools for the people. The number of the children of the Church of Jerusalem in the last three generations did not reach thirty to forty thousands. If the Brotherhood allocated 10% of the income of the Patriarchate, it would have benefited them greatly. However, it did not do anything like that, and we cannot find any trace of such an action. Therefore, I consider that my accusation against them is true."[29]

What was said by this Russian writer is confirmed by history and practice. Both of them testify that the Brotherhood, since its abduction of the spiritual authority in the church of Jerusalem, did not do anything beneficial for the indigenous people of Jerusalem. On the contrary, it would object to anyone trying to accomplish anything useful. But the indigenous patriarchs of Jerusalem were real fathers and good shepherds who did not leave their children for a single instant, in spite of adverse circumstances such as political unrest, the continuous ebb and flow of political power in Jerusalem and Palestine, and the inability of Christian pilgrims to visit the Holy Land. In word and deed, they persisted in comforting both day and night their spiritual children, sharing with them the suffering and affliction. The members of the Brotherhood, however,

---

[29] See "the newspaper of Moscow," N., 346, 1981.

neglected totally the indigenous parishes because the monks were filled with avidity for collecting funds and living in great luxury. Their sole concern was limited to the income of the Holy Places.

This is supported by the fact that at, the enthronement of Germanus, the first Greek patriarch of Jerusalem, peace under the Ottoman domination over Jerusalem was stable in Palestine. Immediately, he neglected his flock and "headed toward Constantinople and other places to collect alms. Upon his return from his trip, he lived in Trans-Jordan where many wealthy Christians were residing."[30] The successors of Germanus, (except for Sophronios), up until Patriarch Cyril, used to elect Patriarchs who would depart this life without ever seeing their flock because they preferred to live in the Jerusalemite Metochion in Constantinople. There they could stay closer to the income producing properties of the Holy Sepulcher in Moldovia and Serbia. For Theophanis, Paysios and Dosytheos, their whole interest was limited to controlling and administering these properties and to traveling in Russia collecting alms. Thus they never asked about their flock and left the task of administering the Patriarchate to a bishop called the "Patriarchal Commissioner." The last

---

[30]-*(Dosytheos, V., 11. Ch., 7., N., 3)*

commissioner in Jerusalem was Meletios, the Metropolitan of El-Tour and the uncle of Patriarch Spyridon. Fortunately, Patriarch Spyridon recovered his uncle's properties after Meletios death.

In 1845, when Cyril, Metropolitan of Lydda, was enthroned as Patriarch of Jerusalem, he moved the headquarters from Constantinople to Jerusalem--not with the interest of his flock in mind, but by a desire to rid of the cupidity of the clergy of El-Phanar. As soon as he arrived in Jerusalem and saw the successful Latin Schools and the printing establishments that they had built to illumine the people, he feared the disintegration of the Brotherhood of the Holy Sepulcher. Its members were sunk in the mud of ignorance, knowing only how to accumulate money, and interested only in dissipation and living a luxurious life. Having a great desire to raise them from that mud, he established a seminary in an old Georgian monastery known as the monastery of El-Musalabah. Although most of the seminarians were from the Greek monks of Jerusalem, they did accept a few indigenous seminarians, but they were not treated equally. They allowed the Greek monks to finish a six-year period of education, while the indigenous seminarians were allowed to only finish a four-year period. After graduating from the seminary, the Greeks were obliged to be tonsured as monks, while the indigenous seminarians were appointed as teachers in the villages of Palestine. Later, only after they married, they were ordained to the priesthood, if they choose.[31]

We do not deny that Patriarch Cyril founded some elementary schools in Palestine, as well as an Arabic printing house and a hospital. However, his accomplishments were little in comparison to the income of the Patriarchate, which in his days, as we saw in the previous chapter, reached millions. Indeed, he was called the Father of Gold! His objective was to elevate the stature of the Brotherhood in the eyes of the people. His accomplishments, which were aimed more at benefiting the monks than the indigenous people, enraged the monks for they saw it as a betrayal of their ethnic policy in Jerusalem and Palestine. For this reason they sought an opportunity to take their revenge on him.

During that same time, the Bulgarian people were rapidly liberating themselves from the oppression and tyranny of the monks of El-Phanar. The monks of El-Phanar were of course enraged at the Bulgarian resistance. But instead of giving in for the sake of the Church and avoiding the schism of a great nation of

---

[31] *See the administrative laws of Al-Mousalba school, printed in Greek 1884, C., 23, 24.*

over five million, they decided to separate the Bulgarians from the Orthodox Church because of their own ethnic interest. And so they held a Synod in 1872 in Constantinople which was attended by four Greek patriarchs. But the rest of the Orthodox churches refused to attend because they knew that the intention was to divide the Church.

At the meeting, the Patriarch of Constantinople and his Synod were able to draw the Patriarch of Alexandria and the Patriarch of Antioch to his side, though the latter sided with the monks of El-Phanar without the knowledge of the Antiochian Synod. Cyril, the Patriarch of Jerusalem, however, did not agree with the other patriarchs on excommunicating the Bulgarians. Mind you, this was not out of his love for justice, but out of his fear that he would offend the Russian church and that the Russian government would confiscate the properties of the Holy Sepulcher in Serbia and the Caucasus. Taking full advantage of this, the monks of Jerusalem embarked upon accusing their Patriarch, Cyril, of partiality toward the Russians. With the support of the monks of El-Phanar, they were able to dethrone him, and to elect Procopios to take his place.

Upon his enthronement, Procopios launched an attack against the indigenous people to please his brothers, the monks of

Jerusalem. He closed down all the elementary schools which had been opened by Cyril as well as the seminary of El-Musalabah. But his attack was not limited to closing schools, he also threw out all the indigenous poor people from the homes belonging to the Church. He launched all kinds of persecutions against the rest of the people by reporting them to the government as being Russian partisans.

The behavior of his successors, Irotheos and Nikodemos, was not any better. The seminary which had been re-opened by Irotheos was closed by Nikodemos on the pretext that the Patriarchate was financially constrained. But the truth of the matter is that he defaulted on his grand promises to the Russian government, which had supported his election as Patriarch of Jerusalem and had returned to him the income from the properties of the Holy Sepulcher in Serbia. Those properties had been confiscated at the time of Procopios who had pledged to devote his attention promoting education among the people and ameliorating their religious and spiritual poverty.

Supporting our assertion that the Brotherhood of the Holy Sepulcher since its inception has not only neglected the needs of the indigenous children of the church of Jerusalem, but continues to use every means to weaken and annihilate them ,is the testimony of the Russian writer Michael Eslaviov: "The spirit of Greek ethnicity has blinded the eyes of the Brotherhood to a degree that they wish that all Orthodox people might join the Roman Catholic church or any Protestant denomination, so that they could make themselves messengers without a local congregation, just like the Armenians. Then they would be able to have complete dominion over the income of the Holy Sepulcher and all the Holy Places. But due to their blindness, they missed the fact that the annihilation of the local community would bring misfortune upon them, for the existence of the Patriarch and the Patriarchate depends upon the people. The desire of the Brotherhood is apparently to make all the twenty five or twenty seven thousand "farmers"--the precious remnants of the old Christian faith--converts to the Latin or Protestant churches, who would generously give in order to attract the indigenous flock to them, so they can establish their own flock from them. At that moment the Orthodox patriarchate in Jerusalem would lose its only support and disintegrate. Since at that time the Greek monks of Jerusalem were really not considered to be the clergy of the church of Jerusalem, but Greek messengers."[32]

---

[32] *The Holy Land and the Orthodox Palestinian Imperial society. pages 86-87.*

*The reader should not imagine that the intention of the Brotherhood is to serve Hellenism in Jerusalem and Palestine. God forbid! If its intention was to serve Hellenism, it would have been using, from its inception until now, all material means to promote Greek education by establishing schools and other centers of education for instructing the indigenous youth, not only in Palestine, but in Syria and Egypt as well. through the establishment of schools and centers of education for the instruction of the indigenous youth.* Although the Brotherhood has not accomplished anything positive, it is still obstructing the children of the Jerusalemite church and the Antiochian church from scholarship but making every effort to leave the native people in a state of illiteracy and ignorance. Had it not been for foreign schools, American, Franciscan, Jesuit and others, you would not see an Orthodox person in Syria and Palestine literate even in his own native language.

The Brotherhood's intention is to pile up money so that its members can reach the highest ecclesiastical positions and enjoy what is prohibited by religion and conscience. The saying is true that every monk in Jerusalem, from the janitor to the bishop, has only one interest, which is collecting money in every possible in order to reach the throne of the Patriarchate. The greatest example is Spyridon, the present Patriarch of Antioch, who ascended the clerical ladder and became Patriarch, not by his virtues and knowledge, but by the accumulation of illicit wealth.

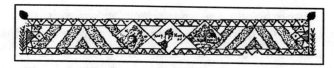

## THE BROTHERHOOD OF THE HOLY SEPULCHER AND ITS RELIGIOUS AND MORAL CONDITION

One of the Brotherhood's oldest methods of making a profane profit is by imitating the Papal church in reproducing indulgences, upon which a picture of the Holy Sepulcher, the Resurrection and some Greek writings are printed, and then selling them to pilgrims. Most Antiochian pilgrims who visited Jerusalem in the middle of this century have these indulgences, which they had bought ignorantly out of simplicity of their hearts. However, the largest circulation of these indulgences have been among the Russian pilgrims. The Brotherhood used to sell to them publicly and without any shame. But when it found out that some knowledgeable and erudite Russian pilgrims were becoming aware of this treacherous exploitation, they started to condemn it in the media. The Brotherhood then ceased to publicly sell them for fear of bad press. However, they kept selling them secretly to unsuspecting pilgrims. Still not being satisfied with this, the Brotherhood legalized many things which are unlawful according to Scripture and canon law, such as baptizing dead babies. Since unlawful things were made lawful by the

Brotherhood, the Russians became infuriated and established the Palestinian Society to take care, spiritually and materially. In essence, the purpose of the Society is to avert Russian pilgrims from the trickery and deception of the Brotherhood.

Truly, the pen resists writing down all the machinations and deeds of the monks of Jerusalem, bloodcurdling even to the atheists. And so we will overlook many outrages, out of respect for the Priesthood . . . But in order to let the reader think that we are not attributing to them things of which they are innocent, we will point out a Greek booklet written by the Greek writer N I Th (printed in Constantinople in 1873) under the title, "The Patriarchal Palace is the Shame of Jerusalem." In this book he demonstrated the life and deeds of some members of the Holy Sepulcher, such as Patriarch Athanasius--the mentor of the late Patriarch Irotheos--and his successor, Cyril, and other monks and nuns whose deeds surpassed the squalor of Babylon and the abominable acts of old Rome. Among other things mentioned in this booklet, the author states: "There was a custom in Jerusalem that each monk had one or two nuns, or even three in accordance with his rank and financial situation."[33]

---

[33] *Page 15.*

If we had left out important historical information for the reader, we would have been satisfied with this single mention about the Brotherhood. A dialogue between Archimandrite Porfiri Ouspensky and Bishop Meletios, the Patriarchal vicar (uncle of the present Patriarch Spyridon), appeared in Ouspensky's diary, printed after his death by the Academy of science in Petersburg in its annual book. The cause of the incident is that a nun under the Metropolitan of Lydda (later Patriarch of Jerusalem). She had a relative who was the grandson of a nun of one of the Archimandrites in Jerusalem. He was an ill-tempered and vicious person. She recommended to David, one the notables, whose wife was a Greek from Adrana, to give his daughter as a bride to the above-mentioned person.

Fearing shame and desiring to protect the honor of his family, David went to the Russian Archimandrite Porfiri, and begged the Archimandrite to protect him from the evil nun of the Metropolitan of Lydda, for she had power and leverage. After listening to him, Porfiri advised him to wait a few days until he found the right time to discuss the issue with the Patriarchal vicar, Meletios. In tears, David answered him: "I can't wait long for they--the nun, with her relative and the Metropolitan--can achieve their desire immediately by banishing me to the monastery of Saint Sabas under the pretext that I am mentally deranged,³⁴ and force my daughter to marry him." These words had a great impact on Archimandrite Porfiri. Then Porfiri reminded him, according to his diary, that the Patriarchs and their vicars in Turkey have some civil authority, for they were capable of punishing the Christians who were under their jurisdiction by banishing them to one of the monasteries or to a penal institution. Thus he decided to go Meletios, the Patriarchal Vicar and implore him to resolve this issue. This took place on June 23, 1884. Unfortunately, since the situation does not allow us to report the whole conversation which took place between Archimandrite Porfiri

---

³⁴ *One of the satanic means which the monks of Jerusalem keep using when they want to destroy any native person who does not agree with them in their malicious goals is to spread the rumor that he is mentally deranged! Thus in Russia they spread the rumor about the devout Archimandrite Christopher Gibarat, and forced him to leave Russia after they deposed him from his office as the head of the Metochion in Moscow. Likewise they did the same with the Metropolitan of Zahle, Garasimos Yared, when he opposed them in electing Patriarch Spyridon. They also spread evil rumors about Gabriel, Metropolitan of Beirut, after all their other various trickeries failed against him. Recently, they spread evil rumors about Archimandrite Seraphim, the head of the Metochion of Constantinople. After deposing him they replaced him with Archimandrite Arsenios. We do not know if they are responsible the bad rumors about Archimandrite Raphael, who was removed unjustly from his office as the head of the Antiochian Metochion.*

and the Patriarchal Vicar Meletios, we will translate only some excerpts. In the discussion with the relative of Cyril's nun regarding David's daughter, Porfiri began by supporting David and his daughter with all his power, saying:

**Cyril:** You have no affection for us and so you defend them.

**Porfiri:** God knows the extent of my love toward you, but I pity the Arabs and I am prepared to defend them.

**Cyril:** They have no faith; they are barbarians, villains.

**Porfiri:** If what you're saying is true, why do you not teach them the Faith? Why do you not make them meek lambs? Aren't you their shepherd?

**Cyril:** They will not listen to us.

**Porfiri:** That is not surprising, for you do not love, but despise them. They are persecuted by all, yet receive no protection from you. They even have nowhere to pray. The village churches are in the most miserable condition.

**Cyril:** You forget that we are under the Turkish yoke.

**Porfiri:** The Turks do not prevent you from repairing and building new churches on the foundation of old churches. And, concerning the decoration of the churches, the Turks do not interfere with this at all. Moreover, there are no icons and vestments in the village churches.

**Cyril:** Where can we find iconographers? We give each priest after his ordination a sticherion, two cuffs, a stole, a phelonion, a disk and a chalice, but they do not maintain them.

**Porfiri:** *(He wanted, as he mentioned in his diary, to answer the bishop by saying that the vestments which they give to the priests are old and used-- nothing else is given to them until their death-- and that it would be better to give them church supplies which are made out of wood and not of tin, but he did not mention these things. Instead he seized the occasion to speak about the moral situation of the priests.)* Your Arab priests do not understand their duties. They perform the sacraments without piety and keep their cattle in the church. Instead of teaching and guiding them, you expel them from your cells as subservient custodians. When they knock on your doors, saying; "Through the prayers of our Holy Fathers," you answer them: "Get out of here, leave, jackass!"

**Cyril:** We do not receive Arab priests so as not to lower our episcopal dignity. The translators inform us about their requests.

**Porfiri:** *(For the first time in my life I heard that receiving a priest lowers the episcopal dignity)* Your eminence, what are you saying? Every bishop is a harp whose cords are the priests. I do not say this, but Saint Ignatius the Godbearer. Witness the great bond which, according to the teachings of the Fathers of the Church, joins the bishop with the priests.

**Cyril:** We do not understand their language.

**Porfiri:** Why not learn Arabic? Your ignorance of the language of your flock is the reason behind the hatred of the Arabs towards you. If you are too old, why not have an interpreter in their presence to forward their requests?

**Cyril:** We cannot introduce new customs.

**Porfiri:** Thus, the old will remain as it is! You do not build schools to educate the children of the priests, and you do not allow the Arab orphan girls, widows and the disabled to find a shelter for themselves in one of the convents. Nor do you allow an Arab to become a bishop, a monk, or even a servant in a monastery.

**Cyril:** This issue does not concern us; it belongs to the Patriarch.

**Porfiri:** *(Seeing that the discussion deviated from the subject which he came to solve, he apologized for his boldness in speaking about the obligations of the shepherds toward their flock. Then he asked him to help solve the problems that David's daughter had with the relative of the nun of Metropolitan of Lydda. Suddenly Porfiri shouted.)* Miserable is the Church which is governed by nuns and not by bishops! If according to the saying of the Lord that everyone who looks at a woman with lust has already committed adultery, how much more sinful if he lives with her? Woe to anyone by whom the stumblings are bound to come! If moral corruption is abominable in the world, how much more must it be in the monasteries and Holy Places!

**Cyril:** *(Listening to these words, Cyril started to fervently defend the practices of the monks of Jerusalem, saying,)* Peter the Apostle was accompanied by a believing wife, and we are his successors. If our Lord Christ permitted himself to be served by women, why should we not accept their service and submission to us? Besides, we were not the first to introduce the tradition of receiving nuns in the mens' monasteries; it is an old tradition. The lesser evil is better than the greater evil. Suppose that, according to your accusation, that we are adulterous, we will be required to give an answer to God . . .

As soon as Cyril finished his terrible defense, the anger of Father Porfiri flared up. He cried out, saying: "Your grace, for the sake of God and the people, if these are your ideas and thoughts, I will say that the kingdom of God will undoubtly be taken away from you and given to others. What else can I say? It will be taken from you. The Orthodox Church has been corrupted because of you and is on the verge of death."

But, have the morals of the Monks of Jerusalem changed in our days? Unfortunately not. Rather their abominations have increased. This what the skilled writer Michael Slaviov states in his book cited earlier:[35] "The existence of beautiful and attractive nuns near the clergy of Jerusalem and all the Jerusalemite monks is nothing out of the ordinary. You can see that these nuns live publicly in the monasteries of monks. The numerous nephews of the bishops and monks of Jerusalem, who are in fact their real children as everyone knows, are the primary source for leadership in the church of Jerusalem."

---

[35]-Page 91-92

Out of respect and honor to our esteemed readers I will remain silent about the most horrible act in the life of the monks of Jerusalem, i.e., pedophilia. If anyone doubts the truthfulness of our statement, let him read the above-mentioned Greek booklet, or the letter of an honored Maronite sent from Jerusalem to the Jesuits in Beirut which was printed in their Good News in 1887.

Knowing just few of the many things about the religious and moral conditions of the monks of Jerusalem, bloodcurdling even to the atheists of our age, we shall hit the nail on the head by saying: "This is the desolating sacrilege in the Holy Place."[36]

---

[36]-*(Matt. 24:15)*

# CONCLUSION

It is clear from what I have mentioned that the Church of Jerusalem had lost after 1534 her importance as an autocephalous Church, becoming with all her properties and income no more than an estate in the hands of a troop of monks from a strange place and land. It did not take long before they formed a Brotherhood similar to a commercial company under the name of the Brotherhood of the Holy Sepulcher in Jerusalem.

This Brotherhood did not limit itself to the embezzlement of the Church of Jerusalem, but embarked upon the abduction of the Antiochian Church as well. Through its wealth, it succeeded in snatching the Patriarchal authority. Given that the indigenous people were aware of its vicious cupidity and malevolent intentions, it used all means and ways through Patriarch Spyridon to eradicate the indigenous clergy and weaken the Antiochian people, so that it might dominate and control completely the Antiochian Church, as it domineered the Church of Jerusalem.

In such a pitiful situation, why isn't every true indigenous Orthodox brokenhearted, upon seeing the trap of devastation set upon his fellow-citizens and the children of his Church by the Brotherhood of the Holy Sepulcher. Why isn't the Orthodox zeal inflamed in him, when he looks at the abduction of the Church of his ancestors at the hands of illiterate speechless person a ravenous wolf who can't understand or be understood. It is only maliciousness that can be expected from a wolf. Throughout history the Antiochian Church has been dignified by honorable hierarchies and righteous shepherds, adorned by knowledge, like Saint Igantius the God-bearer, Ephraim the Syriac, John Chrysostom, John of Damascus, Andrew Bishop of Crete, Sophronius Patriarch of Jerusalem and others from later even periods like Joachim Ghoumah, Michael Hamwoui, Joachim Ibin Ziady Housni, Makarios Ibin El-Zaeim, Athanasius Fadlallah the Damascene, the Priest Michael Breek, the Archimandrite Athanasius Kassir, the Priest Joseph Haddad... Where are the epochs in which the good shepherds and devout monks like Ephraim, Gregory the theologian and John Chrysostom and the others who in spite of their abundant knowledge and virtue, did not dare to accept the staff of pastorship which with one voice offered to them by the clergy and laity, but who rather ran away to the mountains and deserts, considering themselves unworthy to such high ministry? What happened to the past eras and where are we in the present era, where the monks of Jerusalem in spite of the fame of their vices and their immense ignorance do not cease to use all ways, whether they are legitimate or illegitimate, to abduct the hierarchical prominence and snatch the staff of pastorship, against the will of clergy and people, not out of love to serve the Church, but out of avidity to seize authority. They do not seek to serve the flock, but to dissipate the rational sheep of Christ, to collect funds and to live a luxurious life. The saying of Jesus Christ is proven to be true in them: "Very truly, I tell you, anyone who does not enter the sheepfold by the gate, but climbs in by another way is a thief and a bandit. The one who enters by the gate is the shepherd of the sheep. The gatekeeper opens the gate for him, and the sheep hear his voice. He calls his own sheep by name and leads them out. When he has brought out all his own, he goes ahead of them, and the sheep follow him because they know his voice. They will not follow a stranger, but they will run from him because they do not know the voice of strangers . . . the hired hand, who is not the shepherd and does not own the sheep, sees the wolf coming and leaves the sheep and runs away--and the wolf snatches them and scatters them. The hired hand runs away because a hired hand does not care for the sheep."37

Now I say to you, my fellow-citizens and fellow believers: "Why did you turn your face away from the church of your fathers and forefathers, leaving a group of foreign monks striving to destroy you to be a yoke over your necks? Where is your fervor and ardency, where is your honor and love to your Church? Are your hearts petrified and your spirits frightened? Don't you see how the wolves entered your Churches, and your schools were on the verge of eradication? Don't you feel the ignominy and the disgrace, that your Churches were sold, or rather, you were sold to a sly person who shackled your hands and your feet with the chains of spiritual slavery and made you taste the bitterness of colocynth[38] through his misdeeds and tyranny? Arise, Arise, O Orthodox indigenous people, arise from your sleep and hasten to lift the yoke of the Brotherhood from your shoulders and from the shoulders of your brothers. Do not be afraid or fearful, put on the armor of love of your religion and country, do not be branded with the stigma of dishonor and disgrace, for you are citizens in a free Ottoman Empire. The one

---

[37]-*(John 10:1-5, 12-13)*

[38]-*A bitter fruit.*

who does not embrace this Grace is undoubtly a vicious and traitorous person and does not have devout ancestors.